Gifts of Nature

THE JOY OF
SONGBIRDS

Carolina wren and young.

THE JOY OF SONGBIRDS

Marsh wren.

Yellow warbler.

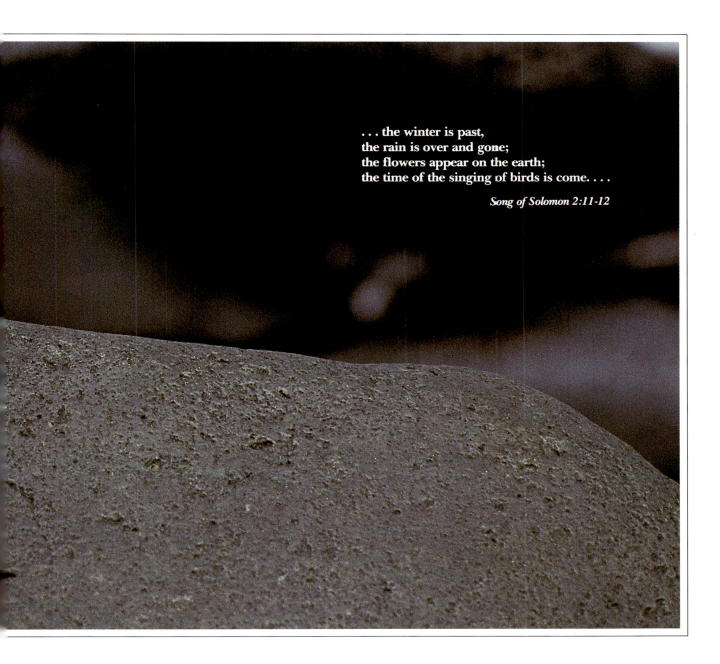

. . . the winter is past,
the rain is over and gone;
the flowers appear on the earth;
the time of the singing of birds is come. . . .

Song of Solomon 2:11-12

A SPELL OF BIRDS

Annie Dillard

For a week last September migrating red-winged blackbirds were feeding heavily down by the creek at the back of the house.

One day I went out to investigate the racket; I walked up to a tree, an Osage orange, and a hundred birds flew away. They simply materialized out of the tree. I saw a tree, then a whisk of color, then a tree again.

I walked closer and another hundred blackbirds took flight. Not a branch, not a twig budged: the birds were apparently weightless as well as invisible. Or, it was as if the leaves of the Osage orange had been freed from a spell in the form of red-winged blackbirds; they flew from the tree, caught my eye in the sky, and vanished. When I looked again at the tree the leaves had reassembled as if nothing had happened.

Finally I walked directly to the trunk of the tree and a final hundred, the real diehards, appeared, spread, and vanished. How could so many hide in the tree without my seeing them? The Osage orange, unruffled, looked just as it had looked from the house, when three hundred red-winged blackbirds cried from its crown.

I looked downstream where they flew, and they were gone. Searching, I couldn't spot one. I wandered downstream to force them to play their hand, but they'd crossed the creek and scattered. One show to a customer. These appearances catch at my throat; they are the free gifts, the bright coppers at the roots of trees.

Blackbird roost, Louisiana.

Song sparrow.

8

A PASSION FOR BIRDS

Roger Tory Peterson

*Y*ou've been out after birds again!" my father snorted. "Haven't you seen them all before? And look at your clothes—nobody with any sense would stay out in the rain." Puzzled, he shook his head. "I swear, I don't understand you," he added reproachfully. I could never explain to him why I did these things; I never quite knew myself.

In my teens, the mere glimpse of a bird would change my listlessness to fierce intensity. I lived for birds. It was exciting just to see them move, to watch them fly. There was nothing thoughtful or academic in my interest; it was so spontaneous I could not control it. In my home town of Jamestown, New York, there are youngsters today whose eyes light up the same way at the sight of a bird. And so it always will be.

A few years ago, on a Tuesday night, during a meeting of my old bird club, the Linnaean Society of New York, I sat in the back of the room where I could see everyone present. There were boys not yet seventeen, men past seventy; several housewives; a man who lived in a hall bedroom in lower Brooklyn and at least two millionaires. One man, unshaven and with gravy stains on his tie, sat beside a distinguished banker in a pin-striped Brooks Brothers suit. A lad of particularly dull intellect sat two rows in front of John Kieran, paragon of quick wit and fabulous memory. What is the common denominator? Here is a challenging opportunity for a group survey by some analyst. Instead of a behavior study of birds, why not a behavior study of bird watchers?

Would symbolism be the key? What do birds symbolize anyway? As with all symbols they probably represent different things to different people. To say that people are attracted to birds because of their color, music, grace, vivacity and that sort of thing is superficial rationalization. I suspect a more fundamental reason is that birds suggest freedom and escape from restraint.

A bird can fly where it wants to when it wants to. I am sure that is what appealed to me when I was in school. Regimentation and restriction rubbed me the wrong way; and the boys in my neighborhood were either younger or older, so I had to dream up my own fun. Birds seemed wonderful things. There were times when I wished that I could fly as they did, and leave everything. When Miss Hornbeck, teacher of the seventh grade, started a Junior Audubon Club, birds became the hub around which my life revolved.

During the first years it was the joy of discovery. Then it became a competitive game, to see how many birds I could identify in a day, to discover rare birds, or to record a bird a day or two earlier in the spring than anyone else, or a day or two later in the fall. This was the listing stage. But as I tore about the countryside, ticking off the birds on my check-list on the run, I gradually became interested in their way of life. At home I pored over ornithological journals like *The Auk*, *The Wilson Bulletin*, and *The Condor*.

As I learned more about birds I found they are not quite the gloriously unrestrained things I had imagined them to be. They are bound by all sorts of natural laws. They go north and south almost by the calendar. They seem to follow certain flyways between their summer and winter homes. A robin that lives in Connecticut this year will not think of going to Wisconsin next year. In fact, we are cautioned by Tinbergen, Lorenz and other behaviorists against saying that birds *think*. We are told they are creatures of action and reaction, "releasers" and responses. A night heron goes through a step-by-step ritual of song and dance. Leave out any one of the steps, and the sequence is disrupted—the reproductive cycle does not carry through. If a female whose legs are still yellowish approaches a performing male she is rebuffed; if her legs are pink she is accepted.

I learned, too, that most birds have "territory." The males hold down a plot of ground for their own—it may be an acre or it may be five. They are property owners just as we are, and song, instead of being only a joyous outburst, is a functional expression, a proclamation of ownership, an invitation to a female, a threat to another male.

Most thought-provoking of all

was to discover the balance between the bird and its environment—the balance of nature that we hear so much about (a swinging balance, it is true), the interrelation that exists between the hawk that eats the bird, the bird that eats the insect and the insect that eats the leaves, perhaps the very leaves that grow on the tree in which the hawk nests. I learned that each plot of ground has its carrying capacity and that predation only crops a surplus that otherwise would be levelled in some different way; hence putting up fences and shooting all the hawks and all the cats will not raise the number of redstarts or red-eyed vireos to any degree at all.

Birds then, are almost as earthbound as we are. They have freedom and mobility only within prescribed limits. It was downright disillusioning to read Mrs. Nice's technical papers on behavior, Kendeigh's studies of environmental factors and Rowan's discussion of migration. But my interest survived this phase and has grown deeper. It has followed the pattern of a thousand other ornithologists I have known. What had started as an emotional release has swung over to an intellectual pursuit.

Reluctant at first to accept the strait jacket of a world which I did not comprehend, I finally, with the help of my hobby, made some sort of peace with society. The birds, which started as an escape from the unreal, bridged the gap to reality and became a key whereby I might unlock eternal things. ◢

Horned lark hatchlings.

Above: prairie warblers; right: yellow-breasted chats.

FINDING GOLD

Michael Harwood

I remember a lovely May morning in Central Park in New York. A friend and I heard an unfamiliar song, a string of thin, wiry notes climbing the upper register in small steps; we traced it to a tiny yellow bird in a just-planted willow tree.

To say that the bird was "yellow" does not do it justice. Its undersides were the very essence of yellow, and this yellow was set off by the black stripes on the sides of its breast, by the dramatic triangle of black drawn on its yellow face, and by the chestnut piping on its back, where the yellow turned olive.

The bird sat at eye level in the middle of the young willow, threw back its head every few seconds, and with puffed-out, vibrating throat, sent its buzzy song straight to the sky.

The low sun perfectly lit this perfect specimen of a prairie warbler—a common enough bird in the East, but one neither of us had seen before.

Having clinched the identification with a quick reference to our Peterson's *Field Guide*, we began a spontaneous jig of exhilaration,

shook hands gleefully—you would have thought we had just found gold—stared at the bird again through our binoculars, checked the book a few more times, pounded each other on the back, danced around in place whooping,

and finally bounced off —no other verb comes close—now and then looking back at the warbler, yet anxious to be on the move, to repeat the experience with some other new bird. I never see a prairie warbler without remembering that event.

The pleasure of adding to one's Life List of birds can be as potent after many years of birding as it is at the start. A favorite story that bears repeating involves the gentleman who introduced me to birds, my father. He chased birds from his teens on, carefully entering the name of each new species in a notebook.

A few years ago I received the following message from him, scribbled triumphantly on a scrap of paper before he left for his office one morning:

*#658   Yellow-breasted Chat
Nov 3 1971
Seen at a distance of 4 feet through corridor window while buttoning shirt.
50 years of patient waiting*

THE NUTHATCH

John Kieran

Out of a clear September sky I was asked by the chairman of the District School Board to undertake the task of teaching the six pupils who would attend the district school that year. The school building was a little unpainted shack in a fringe of woods just east of the railroad cut above Anson's Crossing, which was a "whistle stop" on the Newburgh, Dutchess & Connecticut Railroad. There were half a dozen rows of desks for pupils, one raised desk at the front for the teacher, and a blackboard on the front wall. By virtue of being a college graduate, I was allowed a "temporary license" to teach there, and I went to work at it for the sum of forty dollars a month.

I discovered that rural teachers in that area had to give a Nature Study Course in a small way to their pupils. Part of this program in my term of office included teaching the pupils to recognize four common birds of the region. Colored pictures of the chosen birds, with some pure reading matter attached, were provided by the Department of Education.

When it came time to teach this subject, I picked up the first leaflet and saw on it a picture of an odd-looking bird in what seemed to me to be an utterly impossible position. It was a stumpy-tailed bird about six inches long, white underneath, gray and black on top, and it was pictured apparently going down an old fence post headfirst.

I never had seen any bird proceed in that topsy-turvy fashion and, furthermore, the bird of the picture was a total stranger to me.

I glanced at the pure reading matter under the picture and it ran something like this: "The White-breasted Nuthatch. This common bird is known to every farm boy and girl . . ."!

I looked at the picture again in astonishment. No, sir; never before in my life had I seen anything that looked like that bird, and I had been outdoors in that area for a dozen summers and many weeks at other seasons of the year. Not only that, but the confounded bird was shown *walking down* a fence post, a most irregular procedure in my view.

There was no lesson in Nature Study that day. The bird leaflet went quietly back into the drawer of teacher's desk and I took up some subject I could handle with greater confidence: spelling. I decided that the bird problem could go over until the next morning. I would sleep on the mystery. *La nuit porte conseille.*

As usual, I slept outdoors. My cot was on an open porch facing the east. It was October, with consequent cool weather, and the next morning when I awakened I lingered under the blankets a few minutes before getting up.

About ten feet away on the lawn there was a cultivated Black Cherry tree. As I lay there I noticed something moving on the trunk of the tree. The moving object was, to my

utter amazement, the mysterious bird "known to every farm boy and girl," the aforesaid White-breasted Nuthatch of the Nature Study leaflet—*and it was moving down the tree headfirst!* I reared up on my cot to have a better look at this phenomenon and my sudden movement caught the bird's attention so that it paused in its downward journey to twist its head to stare at me, which put it momentarily in the exact pose of the bird in the picture that the Department of Education had forced upon me. This experience was a stunner and gave me furiously to think. I never had suspected the existence of any such bird until I had seen its picture and a few printed words about it the previous day. But the first thing that met my eyes the next morning was a live specimen of this type not ten feet from the end of my nose!

I decided to begin to look into the matter immediately. It was nearly a mile from our farmhouse to the school and, on the way that morning, I kept my eyes open with astonishing results. I saw four more of these birds going up or down the trunks of trees! By the time I reached the school I realized that I had been practically blind for twenty years. ⋌

White-breasted nuthatch.

15

THE MAGIC OF BIRDSONG

Donald Peattie

For the *why* of bird singing, science has a few answers—none of them complete. One of the most precisely assured is that a bird sings in order to stake out a claim to his bailiwick for nesting. The migrating males, arriving first in the springtime, proclaim each a certain territory as his own.

In some sunny, reedy swamp you may have heard the chorus of the red-winged blackbirds loud in song before ever the streaked females appear on the scene.

"Kon-keree!" they whistle, and it might be translated, at that moment, as "Here am I! Here I stay! This is mine—this patch of reed and sun and water."

As the females come winging from the south, the males sing to win themselves a mate. It is hard to doubt that the females are attracted by the virtuosos among them. And, having won his lady, the male sings through the nesting season, perhaps to please her, certainly because he is so full of the vernal surge of life that it just naturally bursts out in birdsong.

The marvelous spontaneity of fine birdsong is a mystery. Was the wild torrent from the canyon wren's throat once packed away, an inherited gift, in the egg from which he broke? Did the brown

thrasher come by his lovely melodies the same way?

Ornithologists give us a paradoxical answer. It has been concluded that, generally speaking, the simple call notes of a bird are born in him when he is hatched, but that true song may be partly inherited and partly learned, or entirely learned.

Whatever the bird voices that stir you, they are likely to be those you heard early in life, for it is the birdsong of home that has the most meaning for all of us. For many, indeed, there are passages in life scored for accompanying birdsong. For us a shared growing-up in Illinois was full of the rollicking lays of the bobolink, of the contented lament of mourning doves, of the tinkling notes of the goldfinch on his undulant flight—one of the few birds that sing on the wing. Through the years, in many places, runs a musical thread on which dear memories are strung.

There is the ultimate mystery of birdsong—not just the incomprehensible communication between one feathered singer and others of his kind, but the wordless and magical meaning brought to the wondering human senses by a wild, sudden beauty that lifts the heart.

Above: male red-winged blackbird adult; left: juvenile.

17

PRAIRIE SONG

John Madson

Sitting here, gray-haired and Responsible, I can softly whistle the cadence of the western meadowlark and conjure up an instant vision of utter freedom many years ago.

A green-gold morning, the dust cool and soft under bare feet and the road running arrow-straight between fencelines shaggy with bluestem. I am 12 years old, rejoicing in the heady miracle of shedding both shoes and school—hurrying toward the Skunk River and into a summer that had six Saturdays in every week.

There on the fence, dressed to the nines in gold and black and shouting his howdies to every newly freed schoolboy in Iowa, perched a meadowlark. Inspired, I whistled back. My first try was almost perfect, and I've never forgotten how. The western meadowlark and I sang the same song that morning, and we still do.

White-eyed Flycatcher or Vireo,
VIREO NOVEBORACENSIS, Ch. Bonap.
Male.
Vide of China or Pride tree Melea Azederach.

Drawn from Nature & Published by John J. Audubon, F.R.S.F.L.S.   Engraved, Printed & Coloured by R. Havell.

NATURALISTS

In early America, naturalists captivated by birds roamed the fields, marshes and forests, recording their discoveries in illustrations and words. The most famous of these naturalist painters is John James Audubon, whose zeal propelled him to observe and paint birds in all their pursuits.

On a slow flatboat trip down the Mississippi River, Audubon marveled at the voice of the hermit thrush and recorded countless other birds he had never seen before. After he arrived in New Orleans, Audubon painted this watercolor of a white-eyed vireo (*left*) in 1821.

Audubon is the best known early painter of American birds, but others had come before him. Alexander Wilson, a Scottish teacher who landed in America in 1794, taught himself to paint birds such as these orioles (*far right*). It took nine large, unwieldy volumes to hold Wilson's work of art and natural science, the basis for most bird study in America before Audubon's portfolios.

Before Wilson's *American Ornithology,* important art had been gathered in Mark Catesby's *Natural History of Carolina, Florida and the Bahama Islands,* which showed imposing floral patterns such as this flowering dogwood framing a mockingbird *(below).* Catesby, who arrived in America in 1712, laboriously hand-colored many of his engravings.

Oriolus Spurius. Orchard Oriole . 1. *Female.* 2. and 3. *Males of the second and third years.*
4.- *Male in complete plumage.* a. *Egg of the* Orchard Oriole . b. *Egg of the* Baltimore Oriole .

22

PAINTERS

Some wildlife artists have the gift of showing a bird's spirit as well as its physical appearance. Robert Bateman sometimes gives only a glimpse of a bird in its setting, yet the scene gives a feeling of intimacy with nature. This American goldfinch *(left)* is flitting about a meadow full of goldenrod and Queen Anne's lace.

Heather Bartmann's use of subtle shades evokes impressions of Chinese art. Bartman painted this wren *(right)* in the Colorado mountains while it persistently hunted insects.

Bateman and Bartmann are but two of the many modern artists who bring birds to life on canvas. The market for wildlife art is increasing and enthusiasts even have a magazine devoted to the growing field.

BOLD STYLES

Through the years, birds have been admired for their patterns, colors and shapes, and these features have their champions among wildlife artists.

In the 1920s, a West Virginia farmboy stretched out in front of his fireplace on winter evenings making paper cutouts of gulls and rearranging them. Today Charlie Harper still concentrates on shapes and patterns of birds, such as the exclamatory cardinal *(top left)* atop a fresh snowfall. "I don't try to put everything in—I try to leave everything out," Harper once said.

M.C. Escher's artwork features patterns and shapes full of optical excitement. The watercolor "Birds in Space" *(right)* captures the grace of birds on the wing yet challenges viewers to look again.

In her silkscreen of cedar waxwings *(bottom left)*, Susan Hegenbarth distills the essence of the forms and colors in nature.

THE BASHFUL BLUE JAY

Hal Borland

The blue jay is the only bird I know that can be embarrassed. Just to look at him you would never believe it. He is almost aldermanic in appearance, looks solemn as a judge. He is as handsome a bird as you will see. Not spectacular like the cardinal or tanager, not daintily beautiful like the goldfinch. Simply handsome in Dresden blue and snowy white, with a crest to make him look important and a long tail for swagger.

I had known jays only casually, the way most countrymen do, until one spring day quite a few years ago when I had to pamper a badly sprained ankle. Weary of books and an easy chair, I hobbled outdoors to spend an hour just sitting on a sunny bench in the backyard. The apple trees were just opening bud, daffodils were full of bees, forsythia was a mass of golden blossoms. I had no more than sat down when a blue jay out near the barn spotted me and uttered a loud, raucous cry of warning.

Typical. Jays are self-appointed lookouts and sentinels; they warn everybody in the neighborhood when a potential enemy appears, car, crow, man, woman, or child. If they find an owl sleeping in a pine tree, you can hear their uproar half a mile away.

This jay spotted me, screamed the warning, then came to have a closer look. He perched in the nearest apple tree, watched me for

a minute, and screamed another announcement, maybe that I didn't seem to be actively hostile. Two more jays came swooping in, perched in the same tree, and seemed to discuss me with the first one. Another jay appeared, and still another. The five of them hopped from twig to twig, peering at me. Two of them came down and strutted about the grass, inspecting me from ground level, then returned to the tree. They seemed to discuss me several minutes, then decided I wasn't threatening anyone. One by one, four of them flew away. The fifth, which may have been the one that saw me first, though I couldn't say for sure, stayed in the apple tree.

After watching me a long minute, this jay made a quick, intricate flight in the tree. That's right, in the tree, dodging limbs and twigs, circling. Almost an acrobatic exercise as it twisted and sideslipped among the unpruned branches. I had seen that maneuver before

and had marveled at it but dismissed it as show-off stuff. Then this jay paused as though for breath, and a moment later I heard a soft, sweet fragment of song. Very soft, barely a whisper, so soft it was hard to identify that jay as its source. It sang that whisper-song two or three times.

Then I must have moved a hand or even lifted an eyebrow. The jay had been staring at me from only about ten feet away. He turned aside, lowered his crest, ended the song in mid-note. He was the total picture of embarrassment. Then he stiffened, uttered a loud, harsh jeering call, and flew away.

Since then I have heard this whisper-song by a blue jay many times. I know how and when to listen for it. Sometimes it seems to be a mimic song, but I have never heard the full and accurate imitations that others report. I am not questioning them. I am saying only that what I have heard have been fragments of songs I can't identify as I can the mimic songs of a catbird, for instance. And in the spring, when jays are mating, the whisper-song I have heard seems to be unique, maybe a blue jay's love song.

Jays are not openly ardent in courtship. Two males may fight furiously over a female, but male and female do not bill and coo publicly. Perhaps this whisper-song has a part in courtship that we have not yet credited. This is sheer guesswork on my part, but it fits in with the jay's well-known secrecy about mating and nesting. The

nest site is kept hidden, the jays approach it secretly, and nest-building and egg-brooding are very private. The nest is a substantial structure of fresh sticks, not old ones picked up from the ground, plus bark, moss, grass, string, cotton or even paper if available, and lined with fine rootlets. Three to six eggs are laid, pale olive with brownish spots. Both parents incubate, and both feed and care for the nestlings. By late summer and early autumn the family, sometimes as a unit with five or six members, is screaming through the woodland, harvesting and hiding acorns and beechnuts, harassing owls, spotting hunters and shouting the alarm to every grouse, pheasant, duck, squirrel, or deer within half a mile.

Critics call the blue jays brigands, nest-robbers, and murderers. Aside from judging them by human standards—and, don't forget, we raise birds whose eggs we eat and whose plucked carcasses we broil or roast for the table —aside from that, research has shown that the blue jay's average diet is 76 percent vegetable matter such as nuts and seeds, 23 percent grasshoppers, beetles, caterpillars, other insects and their eggs, and only 1 percent eggs, birdlings, salamanders, snails, and such animal life.

I'll buy that. Only once have I seen a jay actually kill another bird's nestling. To me, the whole jay tribe seems to enjoy being considered rascals and tough-guys. But when one of them sings that whisper song and is embarrassed because I heard it, that makes up for all the brazen posturing.

WATER OUZEL

William Matchett

Not for him the limitless soaring above the storm,
Or the surface-skimming, or swimming, or plunging in.
He walks. In the midst of the turbulence, bathed in spray,
From a rock without foothold into the lunging current,
He descends a deliberate step at a time till, submerged,
He has walked from sight and hope. The stream
Drives on, dashes, splashes, drops over the edge,
Too swift for ice in midwinter, too cold
For life in midsummer, depositing any debris,
Leaf, twig, or carcass, along the way,
Wedging them in behind rocks to rot,
Such as these not reaching the ocean.

Yet, lo! The lost one emerges unharmed,
Hardly wet as he walks from the water.
Undisturbed by beauty or terror, pursuing
His own few needs with a nerveless will,
Nonchalant in the torrent, he bobs and nods
As though to acknowledge implicit applause.
This ceaseless tic, a trick of the muscles shared
With the solitary sandpiper, burlesqued
By the teeter-bob and the phoebe's tail
Is not related to approbation. The dipper,
Denied the adventure of uncharted flight
Over vast waters to an unknown homeland, denied
Bodily beauty, slightly absurd and eccentric,
Will never attain acclaim as a popular hero.
No prize committee selects the clown
Whose only dangers are daily and domestic.

Yet he persists, and does not consider it persisting.
On a starless, sub-zero, northern night,
When all else has taken flight into sleep or the south,
He, on the edge of the stream, has been heard to repeat
The rippling notes of his song, which are clear and sweet.

THE PAVAROTTI OF BIRDS

David Hopes

*B*ack when such things were possible I quit graduate school and went to live on a commune in the Maryland countryside. My job there was to serve as community naturalist, my duties vague, in keeping with the times, and centered somehow on giving the students and residents a "sense of the natural world."

It's important to remember that I went there, as I would eventually leave, with a heavy sense of defeat. What I thought of as my academic career had failed, and though I swaggered into the commune bellowing about all I could do for them, the truth was that I had nowhere else to go. I stacked my books around me, jammed my few clothes into the drawers, and lay down to sleep away the half-day drive and the uncertainty of an unfamiliar life.

Sometime before morning I began to dream in threes. Three lights. Three beasts. Three vanished lovers. As I floated toward waking I realized I was *hearing* in threes, hearing something from the daylit world. I jolted awake to realize it was a real bird under my real woods-facing window, a Carolina wren whooping in threes with his little claws tight on a mimosa twig. I watched him for a long while. Each time I moved at the window he flicked closer, daring me to come out and settle ownership of that patch of morning light. I had no way of saying it was his beyond dispute.

The commune wrens were both abundant and aggressive. I had my very own singing under my window, keeping me from slug-a-bedding. Several nested along the thick shrubbery of the main house.

I have a bird book that says the red-eyed vireo is the most abundant bird in the eastern woods. Either that is false or desperately unfair. Think of birdsong as a sort of musical imperialism. If you walk into the forest, you can hear vireos, but those wispy tatters hardly deserve the empire of the wild. It should be the Pavarotti-lunged wren's. I know, I am equating loudest with best. It is a bad habit. But there are uses, such as waking, such as turning the mind from ruts of contemplation, for which plain loudness has no peer.

Now I wake in spring dark, mist heavy from Mount Pisgah above me. Song sparrows bubble from the pine hedge against my window. Cardinals whoop from the clean bare poplars, the mist not softening but magnifying their voices by a thickening of the medium they sing through. It would be structurally apt to say here, "The bird I listen for is the Carolina wren," but there is no need to listen. He blasts through all with his three bells, that amazing decibel from a fluffball lighter than a car key. So he is loud. Loud drives the cat from the nest. Loud makes the predator think twice. The cry of the seraphim is loud, where any hesitancy, any delicacy, is an impertinence. ♪

Marsh wren.

33

THE MOCKINGBIRD

Randall Jarrell

Look one way and the sun is going down,
Look the other and the moon is rising.
The sparrow's shadow's longer than the lawn.
The bats squeak: "Night is here"; the birds cheep: "Day is gone."
On the willow's highest branch, monopolizing
Day and night, cheeping, squeaking, soaring,
The mockingbird is imitating life.

All day the mockingbird has owned the yard.
As light first woke the world, the sparrows trooped
Onto the seedy lawn: the mockingbird
Chased them off shrieking. Hour by hour, fighting hard
To make the world his own, he swooped
On thrushes, thrashers, jays, and chickadees—
At noon he drove away a big black cat.

Now, in the moonlight, he sits here and sings.
A thrush is singing, then a thrasher, then a jay—
Then, all at once, a cat begins meowing.
A mockingbird can sound like anything.
He imitates the world he drove away
So well that for a minute, in the moonlight,
Which one's the mockingbird? which one's the world?

THE DUTIFUL BLUEBIRD

John Burroughs

There never was a happier or more devoted husband than the male bluebird is. But among nearly all our familiar birds the serious cares of life seem to devolve almost entirely upon the female. The male is hilarious and demonstrative, the female serious and anxious about her charge. The male is the attendant of the female, following her wherever she goes. He never leads, never directs, but only seconds and applauds.

If his life is all poetry and romance, hers is all business and prose. She has no pleasure but her duty, and no duty but to look after her nest and brood. She shows no affection for the male, no pleasure in his society; she only tolerates him as a necessary evil, and, if he is killed, goes in quest of another in the most business-like manner, as you would go for the plumber or the glazier.

In most cases the male is the ornamental partner in the firm, and contributes little of the work-

ing capital. There seems to be more equality of the sexes among the woodpeckers, wrens, and swallows; while the contrast is greatest, perhaps, in the bobolink family, where the courting is done in the Arab fashion, the female fleeing with all her speed and the male pursuing with equal precipitation.

With the bluebirds the male is useful as well as ornamental. He is the gay champion and escort of the female at all times, and while she is

sitting he feeds her regularly. It is very pretty to watch them building their nest. The male is very active in hunting out a place and exploring the boxes and cavities, but seems to have no choice in the matter and is anxious only to please and encourage his mate, who has the practical turn and knows what will do and what will not. After she has suited herself he applauds her immensely, and away the two go in quest of material for the nest, the male acting as guard and flying above and in advance of the female. She brings all the material and does all the work of building, he looking on and encouraging her with gesture and song. He acts also as inspector of her work, but I fear is a very partial one. She enters the nest with her bit of dry grass or straw, and, having adjusted it to her notion, withdraws and waits near by while he goes in and looks it over. On coming out he exclaims very plainly, *"Excellent! excellent!"* and away the two go for more material. 🐦

THE BIRDS

Ogden Nash

Puccini was Latin, and Wagner Teutonic,
And birds are incurably philharmonic.
Suburban yards and rural vistas
Are filled with avian Andrews Sisters.
The skylark sings a roundelay,
The crow sings "The Road to Mandalay,"
The nightingale sings a lullaby
And the sea gull sings a gullaby.
That's what shepherds listened to in Arcadia
Before somebody invented the radia.

Female and male barn swallows.

Folk art

Themes from nature permeate the arts produced by the Amish and the Pennsylvania Germans. The stylized birds on this Amish cross-stitch sampler *(right)* are known as distelfinks—literally, goldfinches. They also reflect the interests of the maker, Lydia Smoker, who often put out seeds around her farmhouse to attract birds. The Amish stress humility and avoidance of worldy ways, so Smoker hung her sampler upstairs where visitors couldn't see it.

Birds were likewise a common motif in fraktur, a decorated handwriting used by Pennsylvania Germans on baptismal records, family trees, and other documents such as this bookmark *(left)*.

41

INDIAN CRAFT

Though Indians left few written records, their stories and artifacts reveal that they were fascinated by birds. Adorned with a red-winged blackbird, this painted drum *(below)* was made by a Cheyenne medicine-man. His father had killed four blackbirds with arrows and named his infant son Red-winged Blackbird to give him good luck. More than a foot wide, the drum is made of skin stretched over bent wood and laced with thongs.

A Blackfoot Indian, Green Grass Bull, carved this ceremonial pipe with birds on it *(above)*. The pipe was collected around 1885 by George Bird Grinnell, a noted ornithologist who advocated the creation of "Audubon societies" to focus greater attention on wildlife issues.

The raven, mythical creator of the world and a powerful symbol among Northwest Coast Indians, appears here in a stylized wooden rattle *(below, right)*.

One tale says that a rival of the raven hid the sun in a box; the raven stole back the sun (shown here as a small ball in its mouth), and planned to cast it out to illuminate the sky.

QUILTING

From sunbursts and stars to this stylized songbird *(below)*, reminders of nature found their way onto many early American quilts. The colorful design was made in North Carolina by Margaret Hauser Marion around 1870. Songbird motifs are not common, perhaps because quilters found it difficult to capture a stop-action image of the lively birds on the wing.

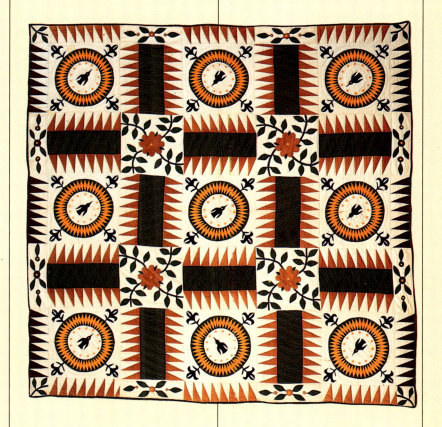

Woodworks

This elaborate wooden birdhouse *(right)* has attracted some colorful carved birds that almost rival the real thing. About two feet high, the birdhouse was made in the late 1800s. Songbirds also have adorned American furniture such as the Pennsylvania pine chest *(right),* made around 1830. The folk sculpture of a songbird *(below)* was carved in the 18th century.

ADVERTISING

Songbirds are so well liked that they have sometimes been chosen for product symbols. These three labels appeared on California fruit crates in the early 1900s. Such labels appeared less often after cardboard boxes came into use during World War II. The images remain so appealing, however, that label collecting clubs have sprung up; original labels now can be worth as much as $600.

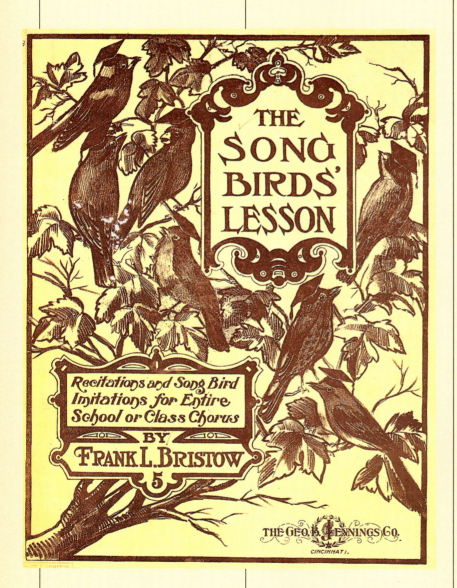

THE SONG BIRDS' LESSON

Recitations and Song Bird Imitations for Entire School or Class Chorus

BY

FRANK L. BRISTOW

5

THE GEO. B. JENNINGS CO.

CINCINNATI.

CHILD'S PLAY

Songbirds have often captured children's imaginations, especially around the beginning of the 20th century. Grade school pupils warbled their imitations of various songbirds during a class lesson *(left)*, and thousands of children treasured stories and paintings of familiar songbirds in *St. Nicholas* magazine and Thornton Burgess' *Bird Book for Children.*

The well-worn robin, wren and sparrow on these painted blocks *(right)* attest to a youngster's hours of play. The manufacturer of a 1914 set of playing cards *(far right)* boasted that the game was "Educational, entertaining." The deck was divided into "familiar birds," "odd birds" and "beautiful songsters," with varying points awarded for each.

CARDINAL VIRTUES

Timothy Foote

*I*t's not that I have anything against cardinals. After all, they sometimes sound as if they'd swallowed Mozart's *Magic Flute*, and in fall, when fiery red males and olive-drab females flutter around together, they can put you in mind of the Red Baron's Flying Circus tangling with a flight of Sopwith Camels.

But when it comes to civic honors and sheer public adulation, enough is enough. Take the official list of 50 American state birds, for example, and the gush of bird books extolling the cardinal virtues.

Any bird fancier at all had to be delighted when the U.S. Postal Service put out its gorgeous sheet of state birds and followed with a glossy booklet full of big bird pictures, small replicas of the stamps, an explanatory text listing state birds and when they were chosen. All well and good, until you look at the feathery lineup a bit closer. A full seven states have chosen the cardinal. Of course there are also

meadowlarks (six), mockingbirds (five), bluebirds (four) and the good old American robin (three). There are some inevitable choices: Maryland's Baltimore oriole; the

Rhode Island Red. Also a pelican (for Louisiana), a gull (for Utah), one television cartoon star (New Mexico's roadrunner), one historic fowl (Delaware's blue hen chicken, the namesake of a Revolutionary War regiment), plus assorted game birds, wrens and thrashers.

But alas, bird lovers, not a single warbler. And not so much as one hawk. Nor a wild turkey, even though Ben Franklin preferred the bird to the bald eagle as a na-

tional symbol: it was "respectable" and good eating rather than majestic, lazy and full of lice.

It's all enough to make warbler lovers and rapturous raptor people cry out for some sort of ombirdsman to guarantee fair play.

The idea of having state birds at all did not catch on until the late 1920s—after heavy lobbying by Audubon societies, schoolchildren and women's clubs. In 1929 in the state of Arkansas, for example, women's clubs put forward the mockingbird. At first, according to Katherine Tippetts, the author of *Selecting State Birds*, the legislature "thought it a huge joke, but when they were given two stirring addresses . . . they voted unanimously" for the mockingbird.

In Colorado, one faction was for the mountain bluebird; another, led by the local Audubon Society, backed the lark bunting. It was sensibly noted that other states had already picked bluebirds, and, in 1931 "when the smoke of political battle rolled away," Mrs. Tippetts reports, the bunting was in by a beak. Meanwhile, down in Florida, despite competition from pelicans, hummingbirds and a large flock of schoolboys who plumped hard for the turkey buzzard, the mellifluous mocker scored again.

The good news for ornithological agitators is that these decisions did not prove irrevocable. After choosing the chickadee in 1933, fickle North Carolina reneged, and a decade later let itself be dazzled by the cardinal.

In Ohio, the jenny wren won popular acclaim in 1928. But five years later a shameless legislature gave the title of state bird to—you guessed it—the cardinal.

Showy beauty of feather and voice played a part in defections. So, perhaps, did the fact that in the past 40 or so years the cardinal has extended its range enormously.

But running through the commentary is a strain of anthropomorphic praise for the cardinal's domestic virtues likely to sway the vote of children and women's clubs. "He is an ideal spouse," says *Selecting State Birds,* "carrying food for the young and finally taking over their entire care."

Alexander Wetmore's *Song and Garden Birds of North America* admiringly notes the male cardinal's "renewed tenderness" toward his mate each spring, his habit of feeding the female when she is incubating the eggs. In fact, the book says, the male cardinal's nurturing instinct is so strong that he sometimes feeds "nestlings of other species." One even took to stuffing the mouths of hungry young goldfish in a nearby pond!

Whatever the merits of such a feathered workadaddy, do we really need seven state-bird cardinals as role models? Other, tougher bird qualities may be worthy of attention.

Nothing perverse, of course.

Nobody would urge the candidacy of the cowbird, whose survival strategy has led it to lay eggs in smaller birds' nests so they'll take care of its kids.

But what about hawks? They are the preeminent flyers of a land in love with speed and power. It was after watching a hawk sky diving that Thoreau wrote: "It was not lonely, but made all the earth lonely beneath it."

Perhaps it's time to celebrate some good old Yankee thrift, too, as exemplified by putting food by for the future. What bird best embodies this frugal approach to life? What bird ingeniously hangs the surplus of its daily prey on thornbushes to provide for leaner days ahead? Let's hear it for the northern shrike. In its pale gray business suit, with offwhite shirt front and handsome black trim, no savings bank—or economy-minded state—could have a better feathered emblem. ✒

...capped chickadee.

A WINTER COMPANION

Dion Henderson

*I*n winter the ax bites sharply into a tree, and toward it hastens the chickadee.

The ax on the kindling in the woodshed has no such effect, with its thuds and ragged sounds of splinters. But in the woods, if there is the crack of wood struck and the steely tone of the ax, presently there is black-capped company come to dine.

Dining, it is well to remember, is the serious business that brought the company, with bib tidily in place. Chickadees learn early that the sound of an ax on a tree may mean a treasure of ants disclosed in the hollow of a rotten oak, or a locust tree riddled by borer and full now of all sorts of frosty tidbits for the probing beak.

I can forgive this forthright greediness more easily than many another gaucherie by a friend, because it is based soundly on necessity and carried off with grace. If the luck is all bad, and the fallen tree is only a box elder with scarcely a hibernating spider to be found, the chickadee will do a day's duty as gay company anyhow, as though it did not matter.

But of course it does.

The chickadee will eat insects if he can, and seeds if he can't, and crumbs if there are neither; and if all fails, he dies, rather easily. Despite the fact that the little black-capped fellow is a creature of our winters, he is not ideally equipped to stand the strain. His heating system must burn more brightly and use more fuel than the other winter birds. To live, a chickadee must stay fed, and dry as well, and out of the wind.

That is why he comes so quickly to join me in the bright, wintry woods, and will follow me all day in the sun, but will not follow me across the open space where the wind may get behind him. And that is why a chickadee will not come to a feeder that faces the wind; he dare not. It is why he must have heavy cover against the damp cold, and be clear of January thaws, and have a hollow birch or shaggy hickory to hide in. This bright and cheerful bit of fluff has few enemies in the wild, except the wind that comes from the northwest by night and searches out foolish little birds that strayed too far by day.

At this time of year the chickadee makes the call that gives him his name, which he is willing to exchange with his listener at length, in tones ranging from the solemn to pure banter. He has a song or two as well, but saves them for their season: the spring whistle of two notes, and another of three that I think is more often heard in the fall.

In the summer the chickadee is easy to overlook. But in the winter, when a fellow needs a friend and is close to woods where the snow is brilliant in the sun, and a dead tree stands stark against the blue-and-white sky, he need only lift the ax and sound the dinner bell.

A CHRISTMAS RIDDLE

Robert Arbib

The Christmas tree, a full and shapely Scotch pine, the snow brushed from its boughs, secure in its stand, was carried from the yard and placed in its traditional corner by the fireplace. Upright, its pointed tip almost touched the ceiling. Perfect!

Suddenly the room was flooded with the scent and memory of forested hillsides; submissive, the tree waited for the box of treasured-from-childhood ornaments and twinkling lights that would transform it from something wild and lovely and lost into something joyous and enchanted.

I climbed the stepladder to begin the transformation with the garlanding of lights. And then, as I looked down into the tree, an unexpected darkness, like a secret, caught my eye. A malformation of the trunk, a knot of dead needles? I parted the branches and peered into the heart of the tree. A bird's nest! With something small and pale cupped in it—a speckled egg!

There is an old Scandinavian saying that has somehow made its way to America, that to find a bird's nest in the Christmas tree brings good luck the new year through. I cannot now recall what kind of luck that nest brought, but for that moment and that Christmas Eve,

the beautifully fashioned thing brought a sense of discovery and a lingering delight. A Christmas gift from nature herself; a reminder that this tree sang sweet songs above the soft sighings of the wind; that a family of living creatures had been sheltered here—hatched and brooded and fed and fledged —that this now silent and sacrificial tree had only a few months earlier

been alive, the glinting of its glaucous needles threaded, woven, and shot through with the dartings of flashing wings.

The nest in the heart of the pine brought with it more than the sudden joy of surprise. There was an added bonus of mystery. What birds had built this nest? Who were the landlords of our Christmas tree, the tenants of this hidden home? The nest itself might provide the answer: surely it belonged to a small bird, for its inner cup was no more than two and a half inches in diameter.

Too small for a pine grosbeak or even a pine siskin, but just about right for a brooding warbler. The outer shell was neat and tightly woven, of twigs and fibers and perhaps thin strips of bark. The inner lining of the cup was, as always, of softer materials, to cradle the eggs without piercing them, to protect the chicks from injury and from the elements. Grasses, moss, hair (deer, fox, rabbit?), and one or two

Black-throated green warbler eggs.

feathers were now all matted into a soft felt by use, and by the weather.

Firmly attached to a forked branch close to the trunk of the little pine, it was a compact work of utter artistry, invisible to any observer on the ground, and with clusters of dense foliage above it, to keep it from the eyes of predators aloft. Surely this was a warbler's nest, as the egg itself—the other important clue —seemed to confirm.

But only a few warblers nest in evergreens, and fewer still will nest so close to the ground. Assuming that the pine tree had been harvested somewhere in the northeastern United States or Canada, the list of possibilities could include only ten species: parula, myrtle, Blackburnian, magnolia, black-throated blue, pine, black-throated green, Cape May, bay-breasted, and blackpoll—among them some of the loveliest of all warblers!

The bay-breasted was quickly eliminated; its nest would be loosely constructed, with unkempt tresses of grass trailing from it in all

directions. Blackburnian and magnolia likewise would build a much less compact nest than this. The blackpoll was automatically ruled out because it nests almost exclusively in spruce—and this was a pine. The handsome black-throated blue was considered and then rejected; it rarely builds more than two or three feet above the ground. What about the tiger warbler, the boldly marked Cape May? No, its niche was at the other extreme: up near the tips of towering trees, far above the ground! And as for parula, its trademark would be festoons of gray-green beard-moss, and here there were none.

The choice was narrowed now

to three, all builders of compact nests, all frequenters of pines, all known to build on occasion within six feet of the ground. But of these, the pine warbler almost always chooses a site far out on a limb. And now there were two, and it was for the egg to decide. The tiny, ovate white egg, a faint gloss still burnishing its surface, was etched and decorated with the finest of lilac-rust flecks around the large end, in a perfect wreath.

And here, in Frank Chapman's *Warblers of North America*, we find pictured an egg identical to ours—the egg of the black-throated green warbler! And suddenly, in that snowy winter season, with the nest's builders and occupants long since flown to more provident winter grounds in Mexico, Panama, Puerto Rico, or Costa Rica, the image of that golden-headed elf with the "delicious lazy little drawl" filled and blessed the room. The nest was left in its secret place, the most treasured of the ornaments that year, its beauty all but invisible in the leaf-clad pine. ✦

Black-throated green warbler female and young.

A SMALL BLUE GEM

Henry David Thoreau

What a gem is a bird's egg, especially a blue or a green one, when you see one broken or whole in the woods! I noticed a small blue egg this afternoon washed up by Flint's Pond and half buried by white sand, and as it lay there, alternately wet and dry, no color could be fairer, no gem could have a more advantageous or favorable setting. Probably it was shaken out of some nest which overhung the water. I frequently meet with broken egg-shells where a crow, perchance, or some other thief has been marauding. And is not that shell something very precious that houses that winged life?

Grackle eggs.

ON WOOING MARTINS

Mary Hamman

Since we dutifully stopped spraying swamps behind our farm pond with DDT, we have been plagued by mosquitoes, big Jersey-shore types. "What you need," advised our neighbor, George, a Princeton-trained Bucks County ornithologist, "is a flock of *Progne subris*, purple martins."

On the wing, George said, they may gulp their weight in insects daily. Flies, dragonflies, beetles, boll weevils and, we were told, mosquitoes (if any happen to be handy) are favorites in the martins' diet.

Purple martins (they are not really purple, for the males are violaceous steel blue, the females dingier-looking) love to build nests in protected places.

Come spring, martins send out early-bird real estate scouts to evaluate available properties. Flocks fly to places these males rec-

ommend. We spent the winter building a house to delight the snobbiest scout. It had 30 apartments, each an eight-inch cube, with entrances two inches in diameter, an inch and a half from the floor, and porches with guard-rails to protect the young. The house is made of kiln-dried poplar with solid oak floor, rainproof roof.

George said it must be 20 feet

above ground, in open space at the end of a body of water for martins to swoop over. We cut down several trees near the pond to make an ideal runway. We used a 20-foot cedar post, with metal guards to foil raccoons, snakes and cats. In April it took four men to raise the house in time for the martin scouts. It looked like planting the flag on Iwo Jima.

We settled down, binoculars at the ready, to wait for our martins. April passed, but no martins came. Ditto May and June. George was optimistic. He said the house was too new. The scouts had not found it. Next year, for sure, we'd have our martins.

In the fall we took the house down—a major operation—and though it had had no tenants, sterilized and repainted it. During the winter I read in the *Purple Martin News* (the martin may be the only bird to have a newspaper devoted to its life-style) that they like to eat eggshells. So in the spring I crumbled a hundred dozen shells, saved by eateries in the village, around the pole. Nearby I assembled a pile of straw, twigs, bits of string and mud for the martins to use in their apartments as interior decoration. We followed this complicated ritual for two more years.

Spurned again last spring, we gave up. Let the Midwest go martin-ape. There they even serve a special martin drink, in scouting season, called a purple martini: a normal martini with purple coloring added. The only creatures we know despicable enough to deserve such a concoction are Bucks County's martin scouts.

Some Indians used to call the martin "the bird that never rests."

I'd change that to "never nests," or maybe better yet, "never wert."

Last July we needed a paper notarized and learned that a nearby farmer was a notary. In his backyard, on a six-foot pole, under a tangle of trees, was a ramshackle birdhouse. Every entrance was crowded with gaping yellow mouths, and every few seconds

adult birds arrived with insects. Surely not martins! There's no water! No open ground for a swooping approach! No white paint! No verandas and railings!

"Yep, they're martins," said the notary. "Been coming here for 15 years." We told him about our scientifically built, but scorned, martin house. And told him about our martin newspaper, eggshells, decorating material and our expert, supervising ornithologist.

"Maybe," he said, "Bucks County martins skipped college. Maybe they can't even read. Put your house in the swampy woods. On a short pole. So's you can clean it easy. And don't paint it. Birds don't like paint smell. Don't myself." That's what we're doing this year. "You'll get 'em," our notary-farmer said. Seeing as how martin scouts are such rotten real estate agents, maybe we will. ⌁

Feathers of a thrush, transformed by backlighting from the sun.

THE FLYING MACHINE

Guy Murchie

Can you imagine any better example of divine creative accomplishment than the consummate flying machine that is a bird?

The lungs are not just single cavities as with mammals but whole series of chambers around the main breathing tubes, connected also with all the air sacs of the body including the hollow bones. Thus the air of the sky literally permeates the bird, flesh and bone alike, and aerates it entire. And the circulation of sky through the whole bird acts as a radiator or cooling system of the flying machine, expelling excess humidity and heat as well as exchanging carbon dioxide for oxygen at a feverish rate.

This air-conditioning system is no mere luxury to a bird but vitally necessary to its souped-up vitality. Flight demands greater intensity of effort than does any other means of animal locomotion, and so a bird's heart beats many times per second, its breathing is correspondingly rapid, and its blood has more red corpuscles per ounce than any other creature. As would be expected of a high-speed engine, the bird's temperature is high: a heron's 105.8°, a duck's 109.1°, and a swift's 111.2°.

Fuel consumption is so great that most birds have a kind of carburetor called a crop for straining and preparing their food before it is injected into the combustion cylinders of the stomach and intestines, and the speed of peristaltic motion is prodigious. You may have heard of the young robin who ate fourteen feet of earthworm the first day after leaving the nest, or the house wren who was recorded feeding its young 1217 times between dawn and dusk. Young crows have been known to eat more than their own weight in food per day, and an adolescent chickadee was checked eating over 5500 cankerworm eggs daily for a week.

The main flying motors fed by this bird fuel are the pectoral muscles, the greater of which pulls down the wing against the air to drive the bird upward and onward, while the lesser hoists the wing back up again, pulling from below by means of an ingenious block and tackle tendon.

If you want to see the ultimate in vertebrate flexibility you must examine a bird's neck. More pliant than a snake, it enables the beak to reach any part of the body with ease and balances the whole bird in flight. Even the little sparrow has twice as many vertebrae in its neck as the tallest giraffe: fourteen for the sparrow, seven for the giraffe.

The most distinctive feature of all in a bird, of course, is its feathers, the lightest things in the world for their size and toughness. The tensile strength of cobwebs is great but feathers are stronger in proportion in many more ways, not to mention being springy and flexible. They serve simultaneously as propellers, wings, ailerons, rudders, shingles, and winter underwear—practically the basic equipment of an airport.

They also form a colorful fluid vestment that is changed several times a year, now serving as camouflage against an enemy, now advertising the owner's charms to a prospective mate.

The growth of a feather is like the unfoldment of some kinds of flowers and ferns. Tiny moist blades of cells appear on the young bird, splitting lengthwise into hairlike strands which dry apart into silky filaments which in the mass are known as down. At the roots of the down lie other sets of cells

which, as the bird grows older, push the down from its sockets. These are the real feathers and when the down rubs off they appear as little blue-gray sheaths which may be likened to rolled-up umbrellas or furled sails. Each of these sheaths is actually an instrument of almost unimaginable potentiality and at the right moment it suddenly pops open—revealing in a few hours feathers that unfold into smaller feathers that unfold again and again.

It is hard for the human mind to take in the intricacy of this microscopic weaving that is a feather. There is nothing chemical about it. It is entirely mechanical. If you pull the feather vane apart in your fingers it offers outraged resistance: you can imagine the hundreds of barbules and thousands of barbicels at that particular spot struggling to remain hooked together.

And even after being torn the feather has amazing recuperative power. Just placing the split barbs together again and stroking them lengthwise a few times is sufficient to rehook enough barbicels to restore the feather to working efficiency—by nature's own Velcro action.

The feather webbing is so fine that few air molecules can get through it and it is ideal material for gripping the sky. In a sense the feather is as much kith to sky as kin to bird, for by a paradox the bird does not really live until its feathers are dead. No sooner is a feather full grown than the opening at the base of the quill closes, blood ceases to flow, and it becomes sealed off from life. The bird's body does not lose track of it, however, for as often as a feather comes loose from a living bird, a new one grows in its place. 🖋

Red-winged blackbirds.

TEXT CREDITS

PICTURE CREDITS

Cover: Robert Villani. **Page 1:** Carl R. Sams II/M.L. Dembinsky Photography Associates. **2:** Michael L. Smith. **3:** Rod Planck/Tom Stack and Associates. **4-5:** Jeff Foott. **6-7:** C.C. Lockwood/DRK Photo. **8:** Robert Villani. **10:** Carl R. Sams II. **11:** Jim Brandenburg. **12:** Robert C. Simpson. **13:** T.J. Cawley/Tom Stack and Associates. **15:** Larry West. **16:** Tim Fitzharris. **17:** Robert Villani. **18-19:** John Shaw. **20:** photograph of Audubon art courtesy of Abbeville Press. **21: left,** from *Catesby's Birds of Colonial America,* edited by Alan Feduccia. Copyright 1985 The University of North Carolina Press. Reprinted by permission of the publisher; **right,** Library of Congress. **22:** © 1982 Robert Bateman. Courtesy of the artist and Mill Pond Press, Inc., Venice, Florida 34292. **23:** art by Heather Dieter Bartmann. **24: top,** art by Charley Harper, photo by Kim Simmons; **bottom,** art by Susan Hegenbarth. **25:** from the collection of Michael S. Sachs; © 1989 M.C. Escher Heirs/Cordon Art-Baarn-Holland.

26: John Gerlach/DRK Photo. **27:** Stephen J. Krasemann/DRK Photo. **28:** Sharon Cummings. **29:** Mike Blair. **30:** Wayne Lankinen. **31:** Jeff Foott. **32-33:** Tim Davis. **35:** William J. Weber. **36:** Robert Lankinen. **37:** John Trott. **38-39:** Stephen J. Krasemann/DRK Photo. **40:** Courtesy, The Henry Francis du Pont Winterthur Museum. **41:** reprinted by permission of Good Books. **42: top,** Peabody Museum of Natural History, Yale University, catalogue no. YPM 1986; **bottom right,** © Steve Myers, A.M.N.H. catalogue #16/292; **left,** catalogue no. 397807, Department of Anthropology, Smithsonian Institution. **43:** courtesy of North Carolina Quilt Project; photographed by Mark Weinkle and Greg Plachta. **44: top and bottom left,** from the collections of Henry Ford Museum & Greenfield Village; **bottom right,** from the permanent collection of the Museum of American Folk Art, New York City. **45 all:** with permission from Out of the West. **46:** Library of Congress. **47:** Courtesy of Washington Doll's House & Toy Museum, photo by Ed Castle. **48:** Carl R. Sams II/M.L. Dembinsky Photography Associates. **49:** © 1982 U.S. Postal Service. Reproduced with permission. **50:** George Stewart. **52-53 all:** Hal Harrison/Grant Heilman Photography. **54-55:** Steve Bertsen. **56:** Leonard Lee Rue III. **57:** John Gerlach. **58-59:** David Cavagnaro. **60:** David Cavagnaro/Peter Arnold, Inc. **61:** Frans Lanting/Minden Pictures.

Library of Congress Cataloging-in-Publication Data

The Joy of songbirds.
    p. cm. — (Gifts of nature)
    ISBN 0-945051-15-8
    1. Birds—United States.
2. Bird watching—United States.
3. Birds in art. 4. Nature
stories. I. National Wildlife
Federation. II. Title: Songbirds.
III. Series.
QL682.J68 1990
598.8'0973—dc20   89-48025
                                         CIP

Printed in Italy.

STAFF FOR THIS BOOK

Howard Robinson, *Editorial Director*

Elaine S. Furlow, *Senior Editor*

Donna Miller, *Design Director*

Debby Anker, *Designer*

Bonnie Stutski, *Picture Editor*

Michele Morris, *Research Editor*

Cei Richardson, *Editorial Assistant*

Karen Stephens, *Editorial Secretary*

Kathleen Furey, *Production Artist*

Paul Wirth, *Quality Control*

Margaret E. Wolf, *Permissions Editor*

Working for the Nature of Tomorrow.
NATIONAL WILDLIFE FEDERATION
1400 Sixteenth Street, N.W., Washington, D.C. 20036-2266

NATIONAL WILDLIFE FEDERATION

Jay D. Hair, *President and Chief Executive Officer*

William W. Howard Jr., *Executive Vice President and Chief Operating Officer*

Alric H. Clay, *Senior Vice President, Administration*

Francis A. DiCicco, *Vice President, Financial Affairs and Treasurer*

Lynn A. Greenwalt, *Vice President and Special Assistant to the President for International Affairs*

John W. Jensen, *Vice President, Development*

Gary San Julian, *Vice President, Research and Education*

Kenneth S. Modzelewski, *Vice President, Promotional Activities*

Sharon L. Newsome, *Vice President, Resources Conservation*

Larry J. Schweiger, *Vice President, Affiliate and Regional Programs*

Stephanie C. Sklar, *Vice President, Public Affairs*

Robert D. Strohm, *Vice President, Publications*

Joel T. Thomas, *General Counsel and Secretary*